Babysoft® is a speci

MW00414818

generously-sized ball. This medium sportweight yarn is machine washable and dryable and comes in pastel colors, making it the ideal yarn for baby and children's items.

About Lion Brand® Yarn Company

Lion Brand Yarn Company is America's oldest hand knitting yarn brand. Founded in 1878, Lion Brand Yarn Company is a leading supplier of quality hand knitting and crochet yarns. Throughout its history, Lion Brand Yarn has been at the forefront of yarn trends while consistently providing its customers with the highest quality product at a value price. The company's mission is to provide ideas, inspiration and education to yarn crafters.

BABY BLOCK BLANKET

◀▉■◻◻▷ EASY

SIZE
About 35 x 35 in. (89 x 89 cm)

MATERIALS
LION BRAND® BABYSOFT®
   #100 White 1 ball (A)
   #101 Pastel Pink 1 ball (B)
   #106 Pastel Blue 2 balls (C)
   or colors of your choice
LION BRAND crochet hook size F-5 (3.75 mm)
LION BRAND large-eyed blunt needle

GAUGE
One Square = 7 x 7 in. (18 x 18 cm).
BE SURE TO CHECK YOUR GAUGE.

SQUARE (make 25 – 8 with A, 8 with B, and 9 with C)
Ch 33.

Row 1: Sc in 2nd ch from hook and in each ch across.

Row 2: Ch 1, turn. Sc in each st across.

> **TIP**
> Yarn Storage Hint: One-gallon sandwich bags are perfect for carrying works in progress. Two-gallon bags are a great size for storing projects.

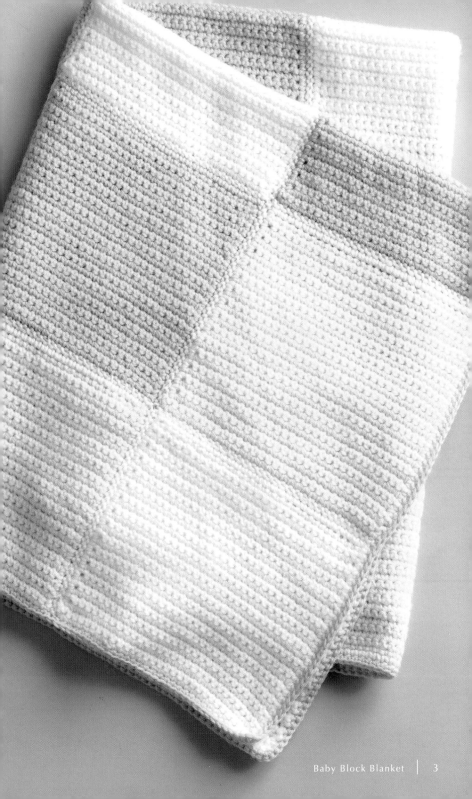

Repeat Row 2 until piece measures about 7 in. (18 cm) from beginning.
Do not fasten off or turn, but continue on to work edging.

Edging
*Work 3 sc in corner, sc evenly spaced along side of Square; rep from * 3 times, join with sl st in first sc. Fasten off.

FINISHING
Following Assembly Diagram, sew Squares together.

Border
With RS facing, join C with sl st in any corner of Blanket. *Work 3 sc in corner, sc evenly spaced along side of Blanket; rep from * 3 times, join with sl st in first sc. Fasten off. Weave in ends.

Assembly Diagram

A	B	C	B	A
B	C	A	C	B
C	A	C	A	C
B	C	A	C	B
A	B	C	B	A

BRAND NEW BABY SWEATER AND HAT

Assembly Diagram page 33.

Shown on page 7.

◀️▮▮▯▯ EASY +

SIZE
One size: 0–12 months

Finished Chest 22 in. (56 cm)

Finished Length 9½ in. (24 cm)

MATERIALS
LION BRAND® BABYSOFT®
  #156 Pastel Green 1 ball (A)
  #100 White 1 ball (B)
  or colors of your choice
LION BRAND crochet hook size H-8 (5 mm)
LION BRAND large-eyed blunt needle

ADDITIONAL MATERIALS
1 button, ⅝ in. (15 mm) diameter

GAUGE
Square = 2¾ x 2¾ in. (7 x 7 cm).
BE SURE TO CHECK YOUR GAUGE.

SWEATER SQUARE (make 38 – 20 with A and 18 with B)

Ch 4; join with sl st in first ch to form a ring.

Rnd 1: Ch 3 (counts as first dc here and throughout), 2 dc in ring, *ch 1, 3 dc in ring; rep from * 2 more times, ch 1; join with sl st in top of beg ch – 12 dc and 4 ch-1 sps.

Rnd 2: Sl st in each st to next ch-1 sp, sl st in next ch-1 sp, ch 3, (2 dc, ch 2, 3 dc) in same sp, *ch 1, (3 dc, ch 2, 3 dc) in next ch-1 sp; rep from * 2 more times, ch 1; join with sl st in top of beg ch.

Rnd 3: Sl st in each st to next ch-2 sp, sl st in next ch-2 sp, ch 3, (2 dc, ch 2, 3 dc) in same sp, *ch 1, 3 dc in next ch-1 sp, ch 1, (3 dc, ch 2, 3 dc) in next ch-2 sp; rep from * 2 more times, ch 1, 3 dc in next ch-1 sp, ch 1; join with sl st in top of beg ch. Fasten off.

FINISHING

Arrange Squares as shown in Assembly Diagram (page 33). Sew edges together through back loops only. Fold Sweater along shoulder and sew sleeve and side seams.

Sleeve Edging

From RS, join A with sl st in seam at lower edge of Sleeve, ch 1, work sc evenly spaced around sleeve edge; join with sl st in first sc.

Next Rnd: Ch 1, sc in each st around; join with sl st in first sc. Fasten off. Rep on opposite Sleeve.

Sweater Edging

From RS, join A with sl st in side seam, ch 1, work sc evenly spaced around all outside edges of Sweater, working 3 sc at each outer corner, sk st at inner corners of neck as needed to keep edge flat and smooth; join with sl st in first sc.

Next Rnd: Ch 1, work sc in each st around, working 3 sc at each outer corner and sk st at inner corners of neck as needed to keep edge flat and smooth; join with sl st in first sc. Fasten off.
Sew button to one top corner of Sweater. Use a ch-sp at opposite corner as buttonhole.
Weave in ends.

HAT CROWN
With A, ch 8; join with sl st in first ch to form a ring.

Rnd 1: Ch 3, work 12 dc in ring – 12 dc.

Rnd 2 and all even rnds: Ch 3, working in front loops only, dc in each dc around; join with sl st in top of beg ch.

Rnd 3: Ch 3, working in front loops only, 2 dc in each dc around; join with sl st in top of beg ch – 24 dc.

Rnd 5: Ch 3, working in front loops only, *dc in next dc, 2 dc in next dc; rep from * around; join with sl st in top of beg ch – 36 dc.

Rnd 7: Ch 3, working in front loops only, *dc in next 2 dc, 2 dc in next dc; rep from * around; join with sl st in top of beg ch – 48 dc.

Rnd 8: Rep Rnd 2. Fasten off.

HAT SQUARE (make 6 – 4 with A and 2 with B)
Work as for Sweater Squares.

FINISHING
Sew Squares into a strip, as follows: B, A, A, B, A, A. Sew ends of strip to form a circle. Easing fullness along strip, sew strip to Crown.

Hat Edging
From RS, join A with sl st in lower edge of Hat, ch 1, work sc evenly spaced around edge; join with sl st in first sc.

Next 3 Rnds: Ch 1, working through front loops only, sc in each st around; join with sl st in first sc. Fasten off. Weave in ends.

EASY-PEASY SWEATER SET

Shown on Front Cover.

◀■■☐☐ EASY +

SIZE
9 months (18 months, 3 years)

Finished Chest: 24 (26, 28) in. (61 (66, 71) cm)

MATERIALS
LION BRAND® BABYSOFT®
> #107 Bluebell 1 (2, 2) balls (A)
> #106 Pastel Blue 1 (1, 1) ball (B)
> #170 Pistachio 1 (1, 1) ball (C)
> or colors of your choice

LION BRAND knitting needles size 9 (5.5 mm)
LION BRAND stitch holders
LION BRAND large-eyed blunt needle

ADDITIONAL MATERIALS
4 buttons, ¾ in. (19 mm) diameter

GAUGE
15 sts = 4 in. (10 cm) in Garter st (k every row) with 1 strand of A and B held tog.
BE SURE TO CHECK YOUR GAUGE.

NOTES
Sweater Set is worked with 2 strands of yarn held tog throughout.

STRIPE PATTERN
Rows 1-6: Work in Garter st with 1 strand each of A and B held tog.

Rows 7-10: Work in Garter st with 1 strand each of A and C held tog.
Repeat Rows 1-10 for Stripe Pattern.

SWEATER
With 1 strand each of A and B held tog, cast on 45 (49, 53) sts. Knit 4 rows.

Next Row: Work in Stripe Pattern, beg with Row 5, until piece measures 4 (4½, 5) in. (10 (11.3, 12.5) cm) from beg, end with a WS row.

Shape Sleeves
Inc 1 st at each end of every RS row 18 (20, 22) times – 81 (89, 97) sts.
Piece should measure approximately 9 (10, 11) in. (23 (25.5, 28) cm) from beg.

Shape Cuffs
Cast on 8 (8, 10) sts at end of next 2 rows – 97 (105, 117) sts. Work even in Garter st and Stripe Pattern for 3 (3½, 4) in. (7.5 (9, 10) cm).

Shape Back Neck
Next Row: K40 (44, 49) sts and slip onto a holder for Right Front, bind off next 17 (17, 19) sts, k rem 40 (44, 49) sts for Left Front.

Shape Left Front
Continue even on Left Front sts for 4 rows. Inc 1 st at neck edge on every RS row 3 (3, 4) times – 43 (47, 53) sts.

Next Row: Cast on 2 sts at neck edge – 45 (49, 55) sts. Work even for one row.

Next Row: Cast on 6 sts at neck edge – 51 (55, 61) sts. Work even until cuff measures 6 (7, 8) in. (15 (18, 20.5) cm). Bind off 8 (8, 10) cuff sts – 43 (47, 51) sts. Dec 1 st at side edge every RS row 18 (20, 22) times – 25 (27, 29) sts. Work even until Left Front is same length as Back. Bind off all sts. Count ridges on Left Front and place 4 buttons evenly spaced between ridges on Left Front opening edge.

Shape Right Front

Attach yarn to Right Front sts at neck edge. Work to correspond to Left Front, reversing shaping and working buttonholes (opposite markers) as foll: work to 4 sts from end of row, (k2tog, yo) for buttonholes, k2 (Front opening edge).

FINISHING

Sew side and Sleeve seams. Fold cuff back. Sew on buttons. Weave in ends.

HAT

With 1 strand each of A and B held tog, cast on 60 (66, 70) sts. Work in Stripe Pattern until piece measures 6½ (7½, 8) in. (16.5 (19.5, 20.5) cm) from beg. K2tog across row – 30 (33, 35) sts. Knit one row.

Next Row: K2tog across, end k0 (1, 1) – 15 (17, 18) sts. Cut end leaving a long tail. Thread tail into large-eyed blunt needle and thread through remaining sts. Pull tightly to secure.

FINISHING

Sew seam. Weave in ends.

Make beautiful and inexpensive wrapped gifts. Wrap the gift in the comic pages of your newspaper and make pompoms from yarns in coordinating colors. Wrap several strands of yarn around the package and attach the pompoms in the center. This gift wrapping is especially dramatic with black and white 'funny' paper and black yarn with a few strands of white mixed in.

BABY TOPPER

■■■▯▯ EASY

SIZES
0–6 months (12–18 months, 2–3 years, 4 years)

Finished Chest 19 (20, 22, 25) in. 48.5 (51, 56, 63.5) cm)

Finished Length 9½ (10, 11, 12½) in.
(24 (25.5, 28, 32) cm)

Note Pattern is written for smallest size with changes for larger sizes in parentheses. When only one number is given, it applies to all sizes. To follow pattern more easily, circle all numbers pertaining to your size before beginning.

MATERIALS
LION BRAND® BABYSOFT®
        #159 Lemon Drop 1 (1, 2, 2) ball(s)
        or color of your choice
LION BRAND crochet hook size K-10.5 (6.5 mm)
LION BRAND large-eyed blunt needle

ADDITIONAL MATERIALS
1 button, ¾ in. (20 mm) diameter

GAUGE
16 sc + 12½ rows = 4 in. (10 cm).
BE SURE TO CHECK YOUR GAUGE.

> **TIP**
> After making a copy of a pattern, use a highlighter after finishing the row. This shows what you have done and what needs to be done on the next row without covering up the last row.

Note: Schematic shown on page 27.

BACK
Ch 39 (41, 45, 51).

Row 1: Sc in 2nd ch from hook, dc in next ch, *sc in next ch, dc in next ch, rep from * across – 38 (40, 44, 50) sts.

Row 2: Ch 1, turn, sc in first dc, dc in next sc, *sc in next dc, dc in next sc, rep from * across.
Rep last row until piece measures 4½ (5, 5½, 6) in. (11.5 (12.5, 14, 15) cm) from beg.

Shape Armhole
Next Row: Ch 1, turn, sl st in first 2 (2, 2, 4) sts, *sc in next dc, dc in next sc, rep from * to last 2 (2, 2, 4) sts, leave last 2 (2, 2, 4) sts unworked – 34 (36, 40, 42) sts.

Next Row: Ch 1, turn, sc in first dc, dc in next sc, *sc in next dc, dc in next sc, rep from * across.
Rep last row until piece measures 9½ (10, 11, 12½) in. (24 (25.5, 28, 32) cm) from beg. Fasten off.

LEFT FRONT
Ch 27 (29, 31, 35).

Row 1: Sc in 2nd ch from hook, dc in next ch, *sc in next ch, dc in next ch, rep from * across – 26 (28, 30, 34) sts.

Row 2: Ch 1, turn, sc in first dc, dc in next sc, *sc in next dc, dc in next sc, rep from * across.
Rep last row until piece measures 4½ (5, 5½, 6) in. (11.5 (12.5, 14, 15) cm) from beg.

Shape Armhole
Next Row: Ch 1, turn, sl st in first 2 (2, 2, 4) sts, sc in next dc, dc in next sc, *sc in next dc, dc in next sc, rep from * across – 24 (26, 28, 30) sts.

Next Row: Ch 1, turn, sc in first dc, dc in next sc, *sc in next dc, dc in next sc, rep from * across.
Rep last row until piece measures 9½ (10, 11, 12½) in. (24 (25.5, 28, 32) cm) from beg. Fasten off.

RIGHT FRONT
Ch 17 (17, 19, 21).

Row 1: Sc in 2nd ch from hook, dc in next ch, *sc in next ch, dc in next ch, rep from * across – 16 (16, 18, 20) sts.

Row 2: Ch 1, turn, sc in first dc, dc in next sc, *sc in next dc, dc in next sc, rep from * across.
Rep last row until piece measures 4½ (5, 5½, 6) in. (11.5 (12.5, 14, 15) cm) from beg.

Shape Armhole
Next Row: Ch 1, turn, sc in first dc, dc in next sc, *sc in next dc, dc in next sc, rep from * to last 2 (2, 2, 4) sts, leave remaining sts unworked – 14 (14, 16, 16) sts.

Next Row: Ch 1, turn, sc in first dc, dc in next sc, *sc in next dc, dc in next sc, rep from * across.
Rep last row until piece measures 9½ (10, 11, 12½) in. (24 (25.5, 28, 32) cm) from beg. Fasten off.

SLEEVE (make 2)
Ch 41 (41, 49, 53).

Row 1: Sc in 2nd ch from hook, dc in next ch, *sc in next ch, dc in next ch, rep from * across – 40 (40, 48, 52) sts.

Row 2: Ch 1, turn, sc in first dc, dc in next sc, *sc in next dc, dc in next sc, rep from * across.
Rep last row until piece measures 7½ (8, 9, 9½) in. (19 (20.5, 23, 24) cm) from beg. Fasten off.

FINISHING
Sew Fronts to Back, sewing 2 (2¼, 2½, 2¾) in. 5 (5.5, 6.5, 7) cm) along each shoulder towards neck. Leave 4½ (4½, 5, 5½) in. (11.5 (11.5, 12.5, 14) cm) at center back neck unsewn. Sew in Sleeves. Sew side and Sleeve seams. Fold about 3/4 in. (2 cm) to right side at end of Sleeves for cuffs; sew in place.

Edging
Join yarn with sl st in lower corner of Right Front; ch 1, sc evenly along Right Front edge to neck, around neck, and evenly down Left Front edge. Fasten off. Sew button about 5 in. (12.5 cm) below neck edge. Use spaces between sts as buttonhole. Weave in ends.

LULLABY LAYETTE

◼◼◼◼◻ INTERMEDIATE

SIZES
Sweater 6 (12, 24) months

Finished Chest 18 (22, 26) in. (45.5 (56, 66) cm)

Finished Length 10 (12, 14) in. (25.5 (30.5, 36.5) cm)

Hat and Booties One Size

Blanket 22 x 33 in. (56 x 84 cm)

Note: Pattern is written for smallest size with changes for larger sizes in parentheses. When only one number is given, it applies to all sizes. To follow pattern more easily, circle all numbers pertaining to your size before beginning.

MATERIALS
LION BRAND® BABYSOFT®
     #107 Bluebell 4 balls
     or color of your choice
LION BRAND knitting needles size 3 (3.25 mm)
LION BRAND stitch holders
LION BRAND stitch markers
LION BRAND large-eyed blunt needle

ADDITIONAL MATERIALS
Circular needle size 4 (3.5 mm), 24 in. (60 cm) long
Circular needle size 6 (4.25 mm), 24 in. (60 cm) long
3 buttons, ½ in. (13 mm) diameter

GAUGE
Sweater, Hat, and Booties: 24 sts + 32 rows = 4 in. (10 cm) in Eyelet pattern with size 4 (3.5 mm) needle.

Blanket: 22 sts + 34 rows = 4 in. (10 cm) in Eyelet pattern with size 6 (4 mm) needle.
BE SURE TO CHECK YOUR GAUGE.

STITCH EXPLANATION
sk2p Slip 1 as if to knit, knit 2 together, pass slipped stitch over—2 sts decreased.

PATTERN STITCHES
Eyelet Pattern (multiple of 6 sts + 1)

Row 1 (RS): Knit.

Row 2: Purl.

Row 3: K1, *yo, p1, purl 3 sts tog, p1, yo, k1; rep from * to end.

Row 4: Purl.
Rep Rows 1–4 for Eyelet pattern.

K1, p1 Rib (over an odd number of sts)
Row 1: *K1, p1; rep from * to last st, k1.

Row 2: K the knit sts and p the purl sts.
Rep Row 2 for K1, p1 Rib.

Notes: Circular needle is used to accommodate large number of sts on yoke. Work back and forth on circular needle as if working on straight needles.

SWEATER
BACK

With smallest needles, cast on 55 (67, 79) sts. Work in K1, p1 Rib for ¾ in. (2 cm). Change to smaller circular needle and work in Eyelet pattern until piece measures 7 (8, 9) in. (18 (20.5, 23) cm) from beg, end with a Row 4 of Eyelet pattern.

Shape Armholes
Next Row: Bind off 3 (4, 5) sts, knit to end of row.

Next Row: Bind off 3 (4, 5) sts, purl to end of row. Place rem 49 (59, 69) sts on a holder.

LEFT FRONT

With smallest needles, cast on 25 (31, 37) sts. Work in K1, p1 Rib for 3/4 in. (2 cm). Change to smaller circular needle. Work in Eyelet pattern until piece measures 7 (8, 9) in. (18 (20.5, 23) cm) from beg, end with a Row 4 of Eyelet pattern.

Shape Armhole
Next Row: Bind off 3 (4, 5) sts, knit to end of row. Purl 1 row. Place rem 22 (27, 32) sts on a holder.

RIGHT FRONT

Work as for Left Front until piece measures 7 (8, 9) in. (18 (20.5, 23) cm) from beg, end with a Row 1 of Eyelet pattern.

Shape Armhole
Next Row: Bind off 3 (4, 5) sts, purl to end of row. Place rem 22 (29, 34) sts on a holder.

SLEEVES (make 2)

With smallest needles, cast on 37 (41, 45) sts. Work in K1, p1 Rib for 3/4 in. (2 cm), inc 6 (8, 10) sts evenly spaced across last row – 43 (49, 55) sts. Change to smaller circular needle. Work in Eyelet pattern until piece measures 7 (8, 9) in. (18 (20.5, 23) cm) from beg, end with a Row 4 of Eyelet pattern.

Shape Armhole
Next Row: Bind off 3 (4, 5) sts, knit to end of row.

Next Row: Bind off 3 (4, 5) sts, purl to end of row. Place rem 37 (41, 45) sts on a holder.

YOKE

Place sts onto smaller circular needle in the following sequence: 22 (27, 32) Left Front sts, place marker, 37 (41, 45) Sleeve sts, place marker, 49 (59, 69) Back sts, place marker, 37 (41, 45) Sleeve sts, place marker, 22 (27, 32) Right Front sts – 167 (195, 223) sts.

Next (Dec) Row (RS):

Join yarn. *K to 2 sts before next marker, k2tog tbl, slip marker, k2tog; rep from * across all markers, k to end – 159 (187, 215) sts.

Next Row: Purl.

Rep the last 2 rows 12 (15, 18) more times, AT THE SAME TIME, when Yoke measures 2½ (3½, 4½) in. (6.5 (9, 11.5) cm), shape neck as follows.

Shape Neck

Next Row: Work first 4 (5, 6) sts in St st (k on RS, p on WS) and place these sts on a holder, work to last 4 (5, 6) sts, sl last 4 (5, 6) sts to a holder. Continue in St st, AT THE SAME TIME, dec 1 st each end of next 2 (2, 2) RS rows.

Next Row (WS): *Work to 2 sts before next marker, p2tog, slip marker, p2tog; rep from * across all markers, work to end. Leave rem 43 (45, 47) sts on a spare needle.

Neckband

With RS facing and smallest needles, pick up and k 61 (65, 69) sts evenly spaced along neck edge, including sts on holders. Work in K1, p1 Rib for 6 rows. Bind off.

Button Band

With RS facing and smallest needles, pick up and k 61 (71, 81) sts evenly spaced along Left Front edge, including neckband. Work in K1, p1 Rib for 6 rows. Bind off. Place markers for 3 buttons with first about ¾ in. (2 cm) from top, last at beg last row of Eyelet pattern, one evenly spaced between.

Buttonhole Band

Work as for Left Front Button Band for 2 rows.

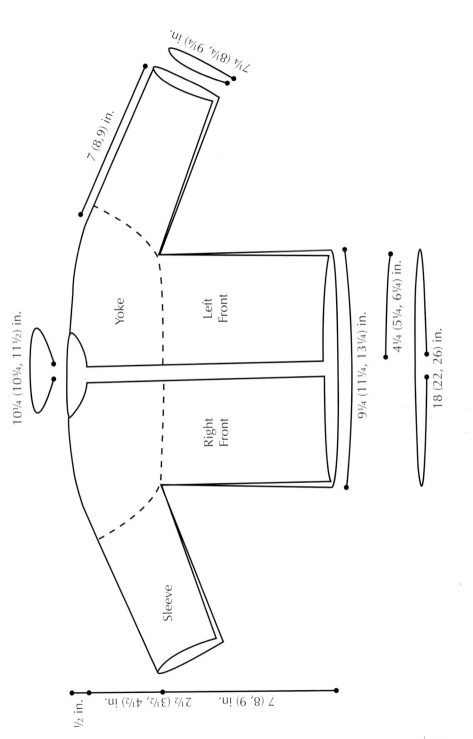

7¼ (8¼, 9¼) in.

7 (8, 9) in.

Yoke

Left Front

Right Front

10¼ (10¾, 11½) in.

9¼ (11¼, 13¼) in.

4¼ (5¼, 6¼) in.

18 (22, 26) in.

Sleeve

½ in.

2½ (3½, 4½) in.

7 (8, 9) in.

Next (Buttonhole) Row:

Work in rib as established, working yo, k2tog opposite each button marker.
Work 3 more rows in K1, p1 Rib. Bind off.

FINISHING

Sew side and Sleeve seams. Sew on buttons. Weave in ends.

BOOTIES

With smallest needles, cast on 27 sts. Work in K1, p1 Rib for 4 rows. Change to smaller circular needle.

Note: Work back and forth on circular needle as if working on straight needles.
Next Row: K1, work Row 1 of Eyelet pattern to last st, k1.
Keeping first and last st in Garter st (k every row) and rem sts in Eyelet pattern, work 8 more rows.
Next Row: Bind off 9 sts, knit to end of row.

Next Row: Bind off 9 sts, purl to end of row.

Top of Foot

Continue in St st on rem 9 sts for 1½ in. (4 cm), end with a WS row. Cut yarn and leave sts on a spare needle. With RS facing and smaller circular needle, pick up and k 9 sts along the bound-off sts; 8 sts along side of top of foot; k across 9 sts from spare needle, pick up and k 8 sts along opposite side of top of foot; and 9 sts along rem bound-off sts – 43 sts. Work in St st for 1 in. (2.5 cm), end with a WS row.

Next (Dec) Row: K2tog tbl, k18, k2tog, place marker, k2tog tbl, k to last 2 sts, k2tog – 39 sts.
Purl 1 row.

Next (Dec) Row: K2tog tbl, k to 2 sts before marker, k2tog, sl marker, k2tog tbl, k to last 2 sts, k2tog – 35 sts.
Purl 1 row.
Rep last Dec Row once
Bind off. Sew back seam.
Seam bound-off edges tog to complete sole.

HAT

With smallest needles, cast on 85 sts. Work in K1, p1 Rib for 6 rows. Change to smaller circular needle.

Note: Work back and forth on circular needle as if working on straight needles.

Next Row: Purl, inc 12 sts evenly spaced across. Work in Eyelet pattern for 24 rows, dec 1 st on last row – 96 sts.

Next (Dec) Row: *K10, k2tog; rep from * to end – 88 sts.

Next (Dec) Row: *P2tog, p9; rep from * to end – 80 sts.

Next (Dec) Row: *K8, k2tog; rep from * to end – 72 sts.

Next (Dec) Row: *P2tog, p7; rep from * to end – 64 sts. Continue to dec 8 sts every row, working 1 st less between decs, until 16 sts rem. Cut yarn leaving a long tail. Thread tail through rem sts and pull tightly tog. Sew seam.

BLANKET

Note: Circular needle is used to accommodate large number of sts. Work back and forth on circular needle as if working on straight needles.
With larger circular needle, cast on 121 sts. Knit 5 rows. Keeping first and last 6 sts of each row in Garter St (k every row), work rem sts in Eyelet pattern, until piece measures 32 in. (81.5 cm) from beg, end with a Row 4 of Eyelet pattern. Knit 5 rows. Bind off.

CLASSIC COVERLET

■■■□ INTERMEDIATE

SIZE
About 34 x 40 in. (86.5 x 101.5 cm)

MATERIALS
LION BRAND® BABYSOFT®
>   #100 White 3 balls
>   or color of your choice

LION BRAND crochet hook size H-8 (5 mm)
LION BRAND crochet hook size I-9 (5.5 mm)
LION BRAND large-eyed blunt needle

GAUGE
14 sts + 7 rows = 4 in. (10 cm) in pattern.
BE SURE TO CHECK YOUR GAUGE.

STITCH EXPLANATIONS
Shell (2 dc, ch 1, 2 dc) in indicated st.

BPDC (back post double crochet) Yo, insert hook from back to front then to back, going around the dc post, draw up a loop, (yo and draw through 2 loops on hook) twice. Skip st in front of the BPDC.

FPDC (front post double crochet) Yo, insert hook from front to back then to front, going around the dc post, draw up a loop, (yo and draw through 2 loops on hook) twice. Skip st behind the FPDC.

AFGHAN

With larger hook, ch 111.

Row 1: Shell in 5th ch from hook, sk next 2 ch, *dc in next ch, sk next 2 ch, shell in next ch, sk next 2 ch; rep from * across to last 2 ch, sk next ch, dc in next ch – 18 shells.

Row 2: Ch 3, turn, shell in ch-1 sp of first shell, *sk next 2 dc, FPDC around next dc, shell in ch-1 sp of next shell; rep from * across, dc in top of turning ch.

Row 3: Ch 3, turn, shell in ch-1 sp of first shell, *sk next 2 dc, BPDC around next dc, shell in ch-1 sp of next shell; rep from * across, dc in top of turning ch.

Row 4: Rep Row 2.

Rows 5–66: Rep last 2 rows. Do not fasten off.

Border

Change to smaller hook.

Rnd 1: Do not turn; working around edges of Afghan, work 131 sc evenly spaced across each long edge, 107 sc evenly spaced across each short edge, and 3 sc in each corner; join with sl st in first sc – 488 sc.

Rnd 2: Ch 1, sc in each sc around, working 3 sc in each corner; join with sl st in first sc – 496 sc.

Rnd 3: Ch 4, sk next sc, dc in next sc, *(ch 1, sk next sc, dc in next sc) across to corner, shell in corner sc; rep from * 3 more times, ch 1, sk next sc, dc in next sc, ch 1; join with sl st in 3rd ch of turning ch.

Rnd 4: Ch 1, sc in each dc and ch-1 sp around, working 3 sc in each corner ch-1 sp; join with sl st in first sc.

Rnd 5: Sl st in next sc, ch 1, sc in same sc, *(sk next 2 sc, shell in next sc, sk next 2 sc, sc in next sc) to 1 sc before next corner sc, sk next sc, shell in corner sc, sk next sc, sc in next sc, sk next 2 sc, shell in next sc; rep from * around; join with sl st in first sc. Fasten off.

FINISHING

Weave in ends.

Baby Topper (Shown on page 12.)

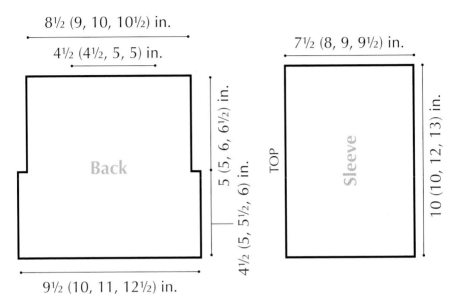

8½ (9, 10, 10½) in.

4½ (4½, 5, 5) in.

Back

5 (5, 6, 6½) in.

TOP

Sleeve

7½ (8, 9, 9½) in.

10 (10, 12, 13) in.

4½ (5, 5½, 6) in.

9½ (10, 11, 12½) in.

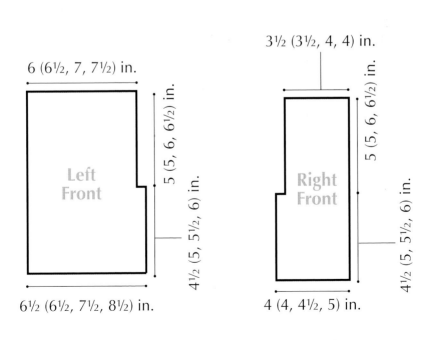

6 (6½, 7, 7½) in.

Left Front

5 (5, 6, 6½) in.

4½ (5, 5½, 6) in.

6½ (6½, 7½, 8½) in.

3½ (3½, 4, 4) in.

Right Front

5 (5, 6, 6½) in.

4½ (5, 5½, 6) in.

4 (4, 4½, 5) in.

GENERAL INSTRUCTIONS

KNITTING NEEDLES		
UNITED STATES	ENGLISH U.K.	METRIC (mm)
0	13	2
1	12	2.25
2	11	2.75
3	10	3.25
4	9	3.5
5	8	3.75
6	7	4
7	6	4.5
8	5	5
9	4	5.5
10	3	6
10½	2	6.5
11	1	8
13	00	9
15	000	10
17	---	12.75

KNIT TERMINOLOGY

UNITED STATES		INTERNATIONAL
gauge	=	tension
bind off	=	cast off
yarn over (YO)	=	yarn forward (yfwd) **or**
		yarn around needle (yrn)

CROCHET TERMINOLOGY

UNITED STATES		INTERNATIONAL
slip stitch (slip st)	=	single crochet (sc)
single crochet (sc)	=	double crochet (dc)
half double crochet (hdc)	=	half treble crochet (htr)
double crochet (dc)	=	treble crochet (tr)
triple crochet (tr)	=	double treble crochet (dtr)
double triple crochet (dtr)	=	triple treble crochet (ttr)
triple triple crochet (tr tr)	=	quadruple treble crochet (qtr)
skip	=	miss

Yarn Weight Symbol & Names	SUPER FINE 1	FINE 2	LIGHT 3	MEDIUM 4	BULKY 5	SUPER BULKY 6
Type of Yarns in Category	Sock, Fingering Baby	Sport, Baby	DK, Light Worsted	Worsted, Afghan, Aran	Chunky, Craft, Rug	Bulky, Roving
Knit Gauge Ranges in Stockinette St to 4" (10 cm)	27-32 sts	23-26 sts	21-24 sts	16-20 sts	12-15 sts	6-11 sts
Advised Needle Size Range	1-3	3-5	5-7	7-9	9-11	11 and larger
Crochet Gauge Ranges in Single Crochet to 4" (10 cm)	21-32 sts	16-20 sts	12-17 sts	11-14 sts	8-11 sts	5-9 sts
Advised Hook Size Range	B-1 to E-4	E-4 to 7	7 to I-9	I-9 to K-10.5	K-10.5 to M-13	M-13 and larger

CROCHET HOOKS												
U.S.	B-1	C-2	D-3	E-4	F-5	G-6	H-8	I-9	J-10	K-10½	N	P	Q
Metric - mm	2.25	2.75	3.25	3.5	3.75	4	5	5.5	6	6.5	9	10	15

ABBREVIATIONS

beg = begin(ning)
BPDC = Back Post double crochet(s)
ch = chain
ch-sp = space previously made
cm = centimeters
dec = decreas(e)(s)(ing)
dc = double crochet
FPdc = Front Post double crochet(s)
hdc = half double crochet
k = knit
k2tog = knit 2 together
p = purl
p2tog = purl 2 together
mm = millimeters
rem = remain(s)(ing)
rep = repeat(s)(ing
rnd(s) = round(s)
RS = right side
sc = single crochet
sk = skip
sk2p = Slip 1 as if to knit, knit 2 together, pass slipped stitch over
sl = slip
sl st = slip stitch
sp(s) = space(s)
st(s) = stitch(es)
St st = Stockinette stitch
tbl = through the back loop
t-ch = turning chain
tog = together
tr = triple (treble) crochet
WS = wrong side
yo = yarn over

* — When you see an asterisk used within a pattern row, the symbol indicates that later you will be told to repeat a portion of the instruction. Most often the instructions will say, repeat from * so many times.

( ) or [ ] — Set off a short number of stitches that are repeated or indicated additional information.

GAUGE

Never underestimate the importance of gauge. Achieving the correct gauge assures that the finished size of your piece matches the finished size given in the pattern.

CHECKING YOUR GAUGE

Work a swatch that is at least 4" (10 cm) square. Use the suggested needle or hook size and the number of stitches given. If your swatch is larger than 4" (10 cm), you need to work it again using a smaller hook; if it is smaller than 4" (10 cm), try it with a larger hook. The same concept applies if you are knitting. If your swatch is larger, work it again with smaller needles. If your swatch is larger, try smaller needles. This might require a swatch or two to get the exact gauge given in the pattern.

METRICS

As a handy reference, keep in mind that 1 ounce = approximately 28 grams and 1" = 2.5 centimeters.

TERMS

continue in this way or as established — Once a pattern is set up (established), the instructions may tell you to continue in the same way.

fasten off — To end your piece, you need to simply pull the yarn through the last loop left on the hook. This keeps the last stitch intact and prevents the work from unraveling.

right side — Refers to the front of the piece.

work even — This is used to indicate an area worked as established without increasing or decreasing.

MARKERS

As a convenience to you, we have used markers to help distinguish the beginning of a pattern. Place markers as instructed. You may use purchased markers or tie a length of contrasting color yarn around the needle. When you reach a marker on each row, slip it from the left needle to the right needle; remove it when no longer needed.

BACK OR FRONT LOOP ONLY

Work only in loop(s) indicated by arrow (Fig. 1).

Fig. 1

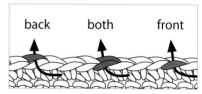

POST STITCH

Work around post of stitch indicated, inserting hook in direction of arrow (Fig. 2).

Fig. 2

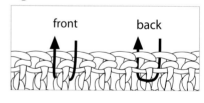

KNIT INCREASE

Knit the next stitch but do not slip the old stitch off the left needle(Fig. 3a). Insert the right needle into the back loop of the same stitch and knit it (Fig. 3b), then slip the old stitch off the left needle.

Fig. 3

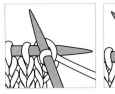

KNIT 2 TOGETHER

(abbreviated k2 tog)
Insert the right needle into the front of the first two stitches on the left needle as if to knit (Fig. 4), then knit them together as if they were one stitch.

Fig. 4

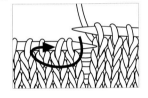

KNIT 2 TOGETHER THROUGH THE BACK LOOPS

(abbreviated k2 tog tbl)
Insert the right needle into the back of the first two stitches on the left needle (Fig. 5), then knit them together as if they were one stitch.

Fig. 5

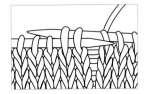

SLIP 1, KNIT 2 TOGETHER, PASS SLIPPED STITCH OVER

(abbreviated sk2p)
Slip one stitch as if to knit (Fig. 6a), then knit the next two stitches together. With the left needle, bring the slipped stitch over the stitch just made (Fig. 6b) and off the needle.

Fig. 6a

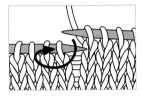

Fig. 6b

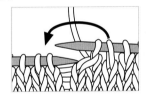

PURL 2 TOGETHER

(abbreviated P2 tog)
Insert the right needle into the front of the first two stitches on the left needle as if to purl (Fig. 7), then purl them together.

Fig. 7

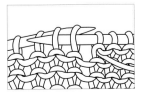

YARN OVER (abbreviated yo)
After a knit stitch, before a purl stitch
Bring yarn forward between the needles, then back over the top of the right hand needle and forward between the needles again, so that it is now in position to purl the next stitch (Fig. 8a).

After a purl stitch, before a knit stitch
Take yarn over right hand needle to the back, so that it is now in position to knit the next stitch (Fig. 8b).

PICKING UP STITCHES
When instructed to pick up stitches, insert the needle from the front to the back under two strands at the edge of the worked piece (Figs. 9a & b). Put the yarn around the needle as if to knit, then bring the needle with the yarn back through the stitch to the right side, resulting in a stitch on the needle. Repeat this along the edge, picking up the required number of stitches. A crochet hook may be helpful to pull yarn through.

Fig. 9a

Fig. 9b

Fig. 8a

Fig. 8b